Smart Animals

WOLVES

by Duncan Searl

Consultant: Karl Kranz
General Curator
The Maryland Zoo in Baltimore

BEARPORT
PUBLISHING

New York, New York

Credits

Cover and Title Page, © Royalty-Free/Corbis; Cover (background), ©Juha Huiskonen/ Istockphoto.com; 4, © Eric Baccega/Nature Picture Library; 5, © Harry Frank, Ph.D.; 6T, © Harry Frank, Ph.D.; 6B, © Harry Frank, Ph.D.; 7, © Harry Frank, Ph.D.; 8, © E.A. Janes/ age fotostock/SuperStock; 9, © Norbert Rosing/National Geographic Image Collection; 10, © Jim and Jamie Dutcher/National Geographic Image Collection; 11, © Daniel J. Cox/Natural Exposures; 12, © Daniel J. Cox/Photolibrary/OxfordScientific; 13, © Monty Sloan/www.wolfphotography.com; 14T, © Daniel J. Cox/Natural Exposures; 14B, © Joel Bennett/Peter Arnold; 15, © David Welling/Animals Animals - Earth Scenes; 16–17, © Daniel J. Cox/Natural Exposures; 16T, © John Hyde/AlaskaStock.com; 17T, © Monty Sloan/www.wolfphotography.com; 18, © Monty Sloan/www.wolfphotography.com; 19, © Monty Sloan/www.wolfphotography.com; 20, © Ronald Wittek/age fotostock/SuperStock; 21, © Daniel J. Cox/Photolibrary/OxfordScientific; 22–23, © Kunst & Scheidulin/age fotostock/SuperStock; 23R, © Monty Sloan/www.wolfphotography.com; 25T, © The Denver Public Library, Western History Collection/Z-1577; 25B, © Stock Illustration Source/Getty Images; 26L, © Jeff Henry; 26–27, © Monty Sloan/www.wolfphotography. com; 28, © Monty Sloan/www.wolfphotography.com; 29, © FogStock LLC /IndexOpen.

Publisher: Kenn Goin
Project Editor: Adam Siegel
Creative Director: Spencer Brinker
Photo Researcher: Beaura Kathy Ringrose
Original Design: Dawn Beard Creative

Special thanks to Dr. Harry Frank

Library of Congress Cataloging-in-Publication Data

Searl, Duncan.
  Wolves / by Duncan Searl.
     p. cm. — (Smart animals!)
  Includes bibliographical references (p.   ) and index.
  ISBN-13: 978-1-59716-370-5 (lib. bdg.)
  ISBN-10: 1-59716-370-8 (lib. bdg.)
  1. Wolves—Juvenile literature. I. Title.

QL737.C22S428 2007
599.773—dc22

                        2006028814

For more information, write to Bearport Publishing Company, Inc., 101 Fifth Avenue, Suite 6R, New York, New York 10003. Printed in the United States of America.

10 9 8 7 6 5 4 3 2 1

Contents

A Wolf in the House 4

Pups and Puzzle Boxes 6

The Fight for Survival 8

Leaders of the Pack 10

On the Hunt 12

Going In for the Kill 14

Staying Close to Home 16

Good Communication 18

Growls and Howls 20

The Call of the Wild 22

The Big Bad Wolf 24

A New Home 26

Just the Facts 28

More Smart Wolves 29

Glossary 30

Bibliography 31

Read More 31

Learn More Online 31

Index 32

About the Author 32

A Wolf in the House

Dr. Harry Frank brought home a new pet. It wasn't a dog or a cat, however. It was a gray wolf **pup** from a zoo.

Dr. Frank was a professor at the University of Michigan. He studied the ways animals behave. He wanted to find out if wolves are smarter than dogs.

▲ **A gray wolf pup**

Dr. Frank's wolf pup was curious about everything. She turned on the water in the kitchen for fun. She made up a hockey game using a flattened coffee can on the icy driveway.

In time, the wolf learned to open a tricky door. First the handle had to be pushed in. Then it had to be turned. Dr. Frank's dog hadn't figured out how to do this in six years!

Wolves and dogs are closely related. Wolves are the **ancestors** of all **domestic** dogs.

▲ **Dr. Harry Frank**

Pups and Puzzle Boxes

To find out more about wolf **intelligence**, Dr. Frank worked with wolf pups and dog pups. In one experiment, he built puzzle boxes. Food was placed inside them. To get the bowl of food out of one of the boxes, the pups had to pull a wooden handle connected to a rope.

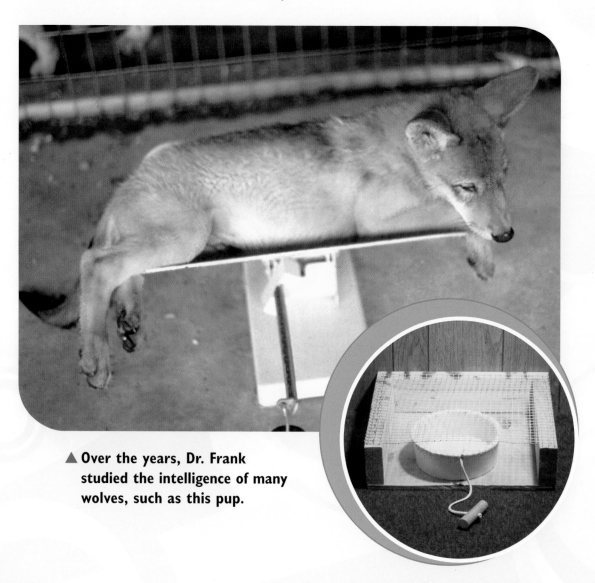

▲ Over the years, Dr. Frank studied the intelligence of many wolves, such as this pup.

▲ One of Dr. Frank's puzzle boxes

The wolves were great problem-solvers. They studied the boxes to figure out how to get the food. The dogs, however, had trouble. Instead of solving the puzzles, many of them begged Dr. Frank for the food!

▲ **Dr. Frank with one of his wolf pups at age seven months**

Wolves are good problem-solvers. Yet dogs are easier to train. After six months, Dr. Frank's wolves still hadn't learned to sit or heel.

The Fight for Survival

In the wild, wolves must solve more serious problems than getting food out of puzzle boxes. Many of them must survive in some of the coldest places on Earth. They must also hunt animals that are larger and faster than themselves.

Solving these problems is not easy. Fortunately, wolves have a smart way to live together—the wolf pack.

Most wolf packs have about 8 members. Some packs, however, have more than 20 wolves.

In some ways, a wolf pack is like a human family. Members of a pack are related. They raise the pups together. They show deep feelings for one another, too. In other ways, the pack is like a well-trained group of hunters.

▲ **The members of a pack show love and loyalty to one another.**

Leaders of the Pack

Two adult wolves, a male and a female, lead a pack. They are the **alpha wolves**. These top-ranked wolves give orders to the others. They decide where to hunt and where to rest. They are also usually the parents of all the pups in the pack.

Next in line is the **beta wolf**. It is the second most powerful animal in the pack. An **omega wolf** is the lowest-ranked member.

▲ **A lower-ranked wolf shows respect by licking the face of an alpha wolf.**

Each wolf knows its place in the pack. The animals use **body language** to show their different levels. A high-ranked wolf holds its head up and its tail straight. A lower-ranked wolf may **crouch** before an alpha wolf. It keeps its tail down or tucked between its legs.

▲ **A wolf may show its low rank by sprawling on its back with its feet in the air.**

Knowing which wolf is in charge is a smart way to live. It cuts down on fighting among pack members.

On the Hunt

Wolves eat only meat. They can eat as much as 20 pounds (9 kg) at one time. To get enough food, a wolf pack has to hunt large animals such as moose and elk. These animals are strong and fast. To catch them, wolves have to be clever.

▲ **These wolves are eating a deer they killed.**

A wolf can live without food for at least two weeks.

Wolves choose their **prey** carefully. They usually look for an old, sick, or very young animal. These weak **victims** are easier to catch.

If the prey fights back, wolves usually leave it alone. That's a smart thing to do. Why risk getting hurt or killed in a struggle with a stronger animal?

▲ **A kick from this elk could break a wolf's rib or leg.**

Going In for the Kill

Wolves work as a team when they hunt. The pack travels many miles together searching for prey. They use their powerful sense of smell to help them find food. Wolves can smell a moose that is more than four miles (6.4 km) away.

In winter, wolves may hunt in single file to save energy. The first wolf makes a trail through the snow so that it is easier for the others to follow.

When wolves spot an animal, some of them might drop down and hide. The others may try to chase the prey back toward the wolves in hiding. They can then surround the prey and attack. Wolves will hunt for hours to find the right victim. Yet they can kill a large animal in a few minutes.

▲ **A wolf has 42 teeth. The four long fangs at the front of the mouth grab and wound prey.**

Staying Close to Home

In the middle of a hunt, a wolf pack may suddenly stop chasing an animal. They do this because the prey has crossed into another pack's **territory**. This area is where a group of wolves live and hunt. Each wolf pack has its own territory. They try not to leave their area, even if it means losing a meal.

When chasing an animal, wolves ▶ can reach speeds of 35 to 40 miles per hour (56 to 64 kph).

The size of a pack's territory ranges from 50 to 1,000 square miles (129 to 2,590 sq km). When there is plenty of prey, packs live in smaller territories.

Having territories makes sense. By staying in their own area, wolves avoid run-ins with other packs. Survival in the wild is difficult enough. Fighting between packs would only make life harder.

The alpha wolf marks the boundaries ▶
of the pack's territory.

Good Communication

Wolves try not to fight within their own packs. They want to avoid **injuries** from biting. So wolves use body language to show their feelings. By **communicating** well with one another, pack members stay on friendly terms.

A wolf may greet another pack member by placing its mouth around the other wolf's **muzzle**.

For example, when a wolf is angry it shows its teeth. It may also curl up its lips. Those signals tell others to stay away.

A lower-ranked wolf that understands this message keeps its teeth covered. It pulls its lips back into a grin. This means "Don't worry. I know you're in charge. I don't want to fight."

▲ The wolf on the right bares its teeth to show it is angry. The wolf on the left flattens its ears to show it doesn't want any trouble.

Growls and Howls

Wolves also use different sounds to communicate with pack members. They bark, growl, **whimper**, and howl. Each sound has a special meaning.

Wolves bark when they are excited or surprised. The sound is often used to warn the pack of danger. A wolf might also bark to challenge an enemy. It's like saying "Back off!"

▲ **Adults use growls and gentle biting to control and teach pups.**

When a wolf lets out a sharp growl, it may mean "Leave me alone!" Adult wolves also growl warnings to pups, such as "Stop begging for food."

Whimpers are friendly sounds. Mother wolves may use a whimper to call her pups or to calm them.

In addition to growling, a wolf might stick out its tongue to show how angry it is!

The Call of the Wild

To communicate over long distances, wolves raise their voices in long howls. The howling is usually begun by one wolf. Soon others join in. It's like a group sing-along. Wolves may howl together for many minutes.

There are smart reasons for howling. Wolves can hear the sounds more than 10 miles (16 km) away. So if pack members get separated, howling is one way to find one another.

Howling also lets two wolf packs know each other's location. It's as if one pack is howling "This is our territory!" Another pack howls back "Our territory is over here!"

Although wolves can howl at any time, they are most often heard in winter at sunrise and sunset. That is the time when the animals are most active.

The Big Bad Wolf

Wolves once lived everywhere in the northern part of the world. Today, they're **endangered**. How did that happen to such a smart animal?

In the past, many people saw wolves as their enemy. People had grown up hearing tales about "the big bad wolf." The animal became a **symbol** of evil.

Gray Wolves in the Wild

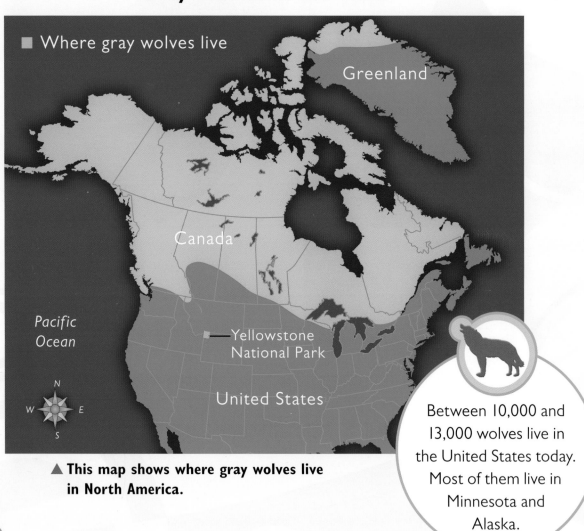

▲ **This map shows where gray wolves live in North America.**

Between 10,000 and 13,000 wolves live in the United States today. Most of them live in Minnesota and Alaska.

Although wolves rarely attacked humans, they did kill cattle and sheep. Farmers wanted the wolves killed to protect their **livestock**. Rewards were often given for each wolf that a person killed. Between 1850 and 1900, more than a million wolves were killed in the United States.

▲ **In the early 1900s, hunters such as this one were paid to kill wolves.**

In popular fairy tales like "Little ▶ Red Riding Hood," the wolf is always shown to be an evil creature.

A New Home

Fortunately, people's views about wolves are finally changing. Instead of killing the animals, many humans are finding ways to help them survive.

For example, wolves had once roamed freely in the northwestern United States. By the 1920s, however, all the wolves in the area around Yellowstone National Park had been killed. Would wolves ever live there again?

▲ **Visitors at Yellowstone National Park watching wolves**

In the mid-1990s, officials at Yellowstone tried an experiment. They released a wolf pack from Canada into the park. The animals did well in their new home. In a little over ten years, more than 160 wolves—about 16 packs—roamed through Yellowstone Park. The new wolves were a howling success!

People from all over the world travel to Yellowstone to see and hear the wolves.

◀ **Yellowstone National Park wolves**

Just the Facts

Gray Wolf

Weight	75–120 pounds (34–54 kg)
Length	5–6½ feet (1.5–2 m), including the tail
Height	2½ feet (76 cm) tall at the shoulder
Fur Color	gray, white, brown, or black
Food	moose, elk, deer, beavers, and rabbits
Life Span	about 8–10 years
Habitat	mainly Alaska, Canada, Minnesota, Mongolia, and Russia

More Smart Wolves

A wolf in an animal **refuge** learned to turn on an outdoor water faucet. When her owner saw the muddy mess, he shouted "No!" The next time the wolf wanted to cool off, the animal turned the faucet on—and off!

A wolf in Alaska discovered a steel trap under the snow. Rather than risk stepping on a hidden trap, the wolf backed out of the area. It carefully placed its paws in the prints it had made when walking in.

Glossary

alpha wolves (AL-fuh WULVZ) the two highest-ranked wolves, a male and a female, in the pack

ancestors (AN-sess-turz) family members who lived a long time ago

beta wolf (BAY-tuh WULF) the second highest-ranked wolf, male or female, in the pack

body language (BOD-ee LANG-gwij) body movements and facial expressions that show one's feelings

communicating (kuh-MYOO-nuh-*kate*-ing) sharing information, wants, needs, and feelings

crouch (KROUCH) to lower one's body

domestic (duh-MESS-tik) bred and tamed for use by humans

endangered (en-DAYN-jurd) in danger of dying out

injuries (IN-juh-reez) harm or damage

intelligence (in-TEL-uh-juhns) the ability to learn, understand, and solve problems

livestock (LIVE-*stok*) animals, such as sheep, chickens, and cows, that are raised on a farm

muzzle (MUHZ-uhl) the nose, mouth, and jaws of an animal

omega wolf (oh-MAY-guh WULF) the lowest-ranked wolf in a pack

prey (PRAY) animals that are hunted or caught for food

pup (PUP) short for "puppy"

refuge (REF-yooj) a place that provides shelter or protection

symbol (SIM-buhl) something that stands for something else

territory (TER-uh-*tor*-ee) an area that belongs to a group of animals

victims (VIK-tuhmz) animals or people who are hurt or killed

whimper (WIM-pur) to make a crying sound

Bibliography

Hampton, Bruce. *The Great American Wolf.* New York: Henry Holt (1997).

Savage, Candace. *The World of the Wolf.* San Francisco, CA: Sierra Club Books (1996).

Smith, Douglas W., and Gary Ferguson. *Decade of the Wolf: Returning the Wild to Yellowstone.* Guilford, CT: The Lyons Press (2005).

Steinhart, Peter. *The Company of Wolves.* New York: Vintage (1996).

Zimen, Erik. *The Wolf: A Species in Danger.* New York: Delacorte Press (1981).

Read More

Becker, John E. *Gray Wolves (Returning Wildlife).* San Diego, CA: KidHaven Press (2004).

Brandenburg, Jim. *To the Top of the World: Adventures with Arctic Wolves.* New York: Walker and Company (1993).

Kalman, Bobbie. *Endangered Wolves.* New York: Crabtree Publishing (2005).

Lawrence, R. D. *Wolves.* San Francisco, CA: Sierra Club Books (1990).

Learn More Online

To learn more about wolves, visit
www.bearportpublishing.com/SmartAnimals

Index

Alaska 24, 28–29

alpha wolves 10–11, 17

barking 20

beta wolves 10

body language 11, 18–19

Canada 24, 27, 28

communication 11, 18–19, 20–21, 22–23

deer 12, 28

dogs 4–5, 6–7

elk 12–13, 28

endangered 24

fangs 15

food 6–7, 8, 12, 14, 21, 28

Frank, Dr. Harry 4–5, 6–7

growling 20–21

howling 20, 22–23

hunting 8–9, 10, 12–13, 14–15, 16

Minnesota 24, 28

Mongolia 28

moose 12, 14, 28

omega wolves 10

prey 13, 14–15, 16

problem-solving 7, 8

puzzle boxes 6–7, 8

Russia 28

territory 16–17, 23

United States 24–25, 26

whimpering 20–21

wolf pack 8–9, 10–11, 12, 14, 16–17, 18, 20, 22–23, 27

Yellowstone National Park 24, 26–27

About the Author

Duncan Searl is a writer and editor who lives in New York. He is the author of many books for young readers.